MARS
A First Look

PERCY LEED

GRL Consultants,
Diane Craig and Monica Marx,
Certified Literacy Specialists

Lerner Publications ◆ Minneapolis

Educator Toolbox

Reading books is a great way for kids to express what they're interested in. Before reading this title, ask the reader these questions:

What do you think this book is about? Look at the cover for clues.

What do you already know about Mars?

What do you want to learn about Mars?

Let's Read Together

Encourage the reader to use the pictures to understand the text.

Point out when the reader successfully sounds out a word.

Praise the reader for recognizing sight words such as *this* and *with*.

TABLE OF CONTENTS

Mars

This is Mars.
Mars is part of
our solar system.

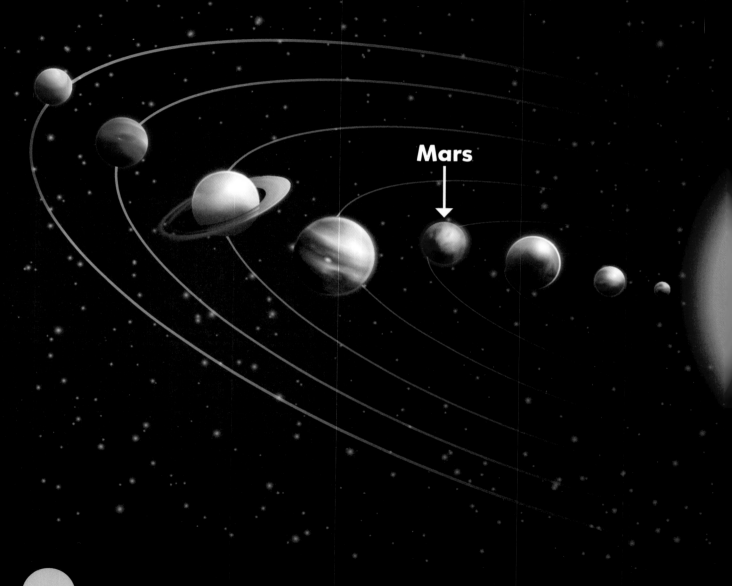

Mars

the sun

Our solar system
has eight planets
and the sun.

Mercury Mars Venus Earth Neptune

Uranus Saturn Jupiter

Mars is the second-smallest planet in the solar system.

It is about half the size of Earth.

Earth

Mars

Mars is known as
the Red Planet.
Its rocks and dirt are
the color of rust.

A year on Mars is
687 Earth days.
This is how long it
takes Mars to travel
around the sun.

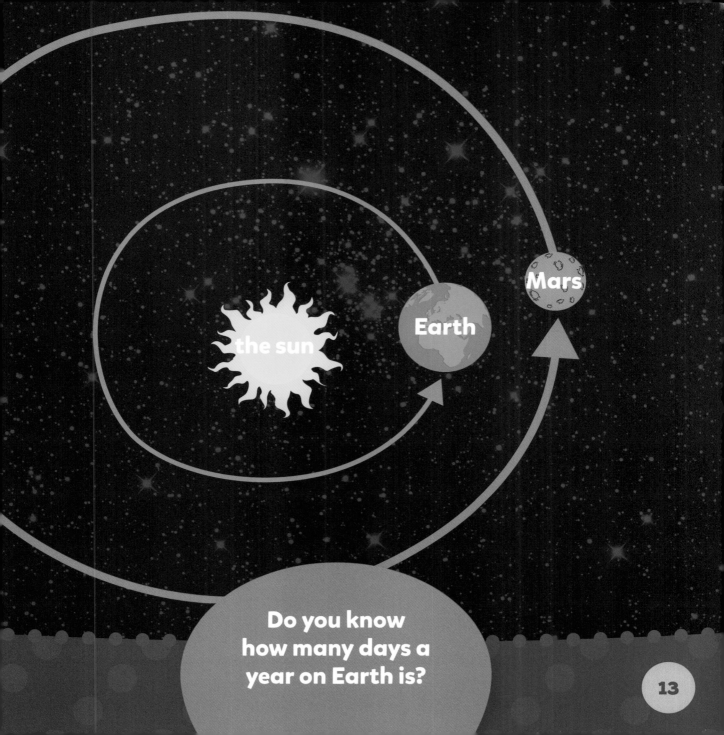

the sun

Earth

Mars

Do you know how many days a year on Earth is?

Mars has
two moons.
Each travels
around Mars
on its own path.

Mars

Do you know
how many moons
Earth has?

moon

moon

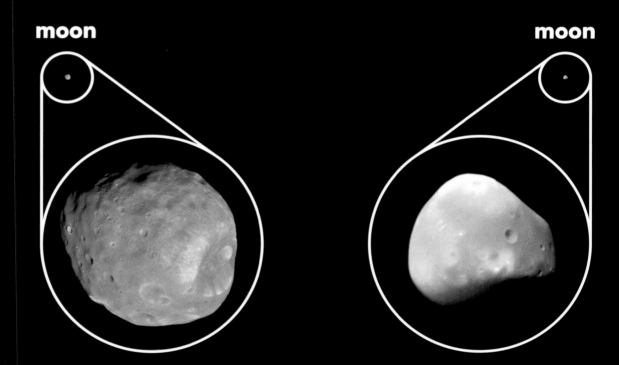

Humans study Mars. They look at the planet with tools called telescopes.

Humans also send robots to Mars. The robots help us learn about the planet.

robot

surface
of Mars

Someday, humans will travel to Mars.
The trip will take about eight months!

You Connect!

What is something you like about Mars?

Do you think you would like to visit Mars?

What other planets do you know about?

STEM Snapshot

Encourage students to think and ask questions like scientists. Ask the reader:

What is something you learned about Mars?

What is something you noticed about Mars?

What is something you still want to learn about Mars?

Photo Glossary

Earth

Mars

moon

telescope

Learn More

McAnulty, Stacy. *Mars! Earthlings Welcome*. New York: Henry Holt, 2021.

Schonfeld, Sara. *Birthday on Mars!* New York: Penguin Workshop, 2019.

Sommer, Nathan. *Mars*. Minneapolis: Bellwether Media, 2019.

Index

Photo Acknowledgments

The images in this book are used with the permission of: © Macrovector/Shutterstock Images, pp. 6–7; © Maria Jose Silva Jimenez/Shutterstock Images, pp. 4–5; © Mascha Tace/Shutterstock Images, p. 8; © NASA, pp. 16–17, 23 (telescope); © NASA/JPL-Caltech, pp. 10–11, 20; © NASA/JPL-Caltech/MSSS, pp. 18–19; © NASA/JPL-Caltech/University of Arizona, p. 10; © NASA/JPL/Malin Space Science Systems/Wikimedia, pp. 15 (moon, left), 23 (moon); © NASA/Wikimedia, p. 15 (moon, right); © Nasky/Shutterstock Images, p. 12–13; © Nbound/Wikimedia, p. 14–15 (main); © Tristan3D/Shutterstock Images, pp. 9, 23 (Earth, Mars).

Cover Photo: © NASA/Kevin M. Gill.

Design Elements: © Mighty Media, Inc.

Lerner Publications Company
An imprint of Lerner Publishing Group, Inc.
241 First Avenue North
Minneapolis, MN 55401 USA

For reading levels and more information, look up this title at www.lernerbooks.com.

Main body text set in Mikado a Medium.
Typeface provided by Hannes von Doehren.

Library of Congress Cataloging-in-Publication Data

Names: Leed, Percy, 1968– author.
Title: Mars : a first look / Percy Leed.
Description: Minneapolis, MN : Lerner Publications, [2023] | Series: Read about space (read for a better world) | Includes bibliographical references and index. | Audience: Ages 5–8 | Audience: Grades K–1 | Summary: "Mars is the fourth planet from the Sun. Easy-to-read text and fascinating photos give readers a first look at the Red Planet"– Provided by publisher.
Identifiers: LCCN 2021045342 (print) | LCCN 2021045343 (ebook) | ISBN 9781728459257 (library binding) | ISBN 9781728464336 (paperback) | ISBN 9781728462189 (ebook)
Subjects: LCSH: Mars (Planet)—Juvenile literature.
Classification: LCC QB641 .L389 2023 (print) | LCC QB641 (ebook) | DDC 523.43—dc23/eng/20211116

LC record available at https://lccn.loc.gov/2021045342
LC ebook record available at https://lccn.loc.gov/2021045343

Manufactured in the United States of America
2-1009739-50270-5/31/2023